T0127308

Sorry, Tree

SORRY, TREE

EILEEN MYLES

WAVE BOOKS

SEATTLE/NEW YORK

Published by Wave Books
www.wavepoetry.com

Copyright © 2007 by Eileen Myles   .
All rights reserved

Wave Books titles are distributed to the trade by
Consortium Book Sales and Distribution
1045 Westgate Drive, St. Paul, Minnesota 55114

Library of Congress Cataloging-in-Publication Data
Myles, Eileen.
Sorry, tree / Eileen Myles. — 1st ed.
p. cm.
ISBN 13: 978-1-933517-20-9
[*Trade Paper*]
ISBN 13: 978-1-933517-21-6
[*Limited Edition Hardcover*]
I. Title.
PS3563.Y498S67 2007
811´.54—dc22
2006038906

Cover design by Neil Stuber
Printed in the United States of America

9 8 7 6 5 4 3

Wave Books 008

for Bob

Contents

Sorry, Tree

When I think
about loving
you
I think
about opening
my bible
and shaking
it

I'm sick
of saving
my love
in prayer books
I've been
such a greedy
wretch

I'm cleaning
a window
with you
I'm grasping
the present
I'm gasping

that honey
that such

light
that such
a gooey
mess
beeping
lights

I feel transparent
I try it again
throwing my
baby against
plastic

I think of
vanishing
in cream

this storm

after a monster
tore down
the town
left on
the doorstep

is us

why

smiling
the world
in our
hands a rattle
such a
joke
we shake it
shake it
shake it

NO REWRITING

nobody's going to come in
and take my cup of money

sometimes the only no I have
is to reverse things

I agree. It's a good place to shit.

This morning it was summer
while I stayed in
I watched spring fade
I went out in chill fall
and walked my dog
in winters   rectangles of trash
striking our face
the wind turning flags and banners
into danger
man the wind was big
in this fragmented
city

I want to be a part of something bigger than myself
not the university of california but it's a start
my dad was a gorilla

who did you think I would be

how do you spell univercity
it always looks cilly

I will think
I will read

I will wake up loving you and when I come home
I will love you.
Look I bought tickets for the movies for tomorrow night
I will buy you a hot dog then you know what

They didn't know I was so great
it was humbling
now it is fine

I sent her this email about the big awards
the paranoia I feel about all the award
winners
now I'm like king of the losers again
I said king king king

it's like genitals
I want to show you all these tiny parts

but I'm public public public

I went to the University of Massachusetts
and for all these years the city of New
York has given me a rent stabilization
grant

and now California golden state opens her
arms to us

come to mama

I wrote this poem twenty-four years ago
but nobody saw it yet
so I'm safe

she said you are such a good boy

that morning I had just moved my car
today on the blue paper the hell's angels flag is
rolled like toilet paper, just a thin stream
of tattered flag thanks to the accident
of weather last night's wind

and I got back in bed and she called
I think the bridges will be closed
and everyone was screaming on the roof
there's another one
no she said I'm watching teevee
so I brought her up to the roof with me
and all my neighbors standing up there the whole block
like history and it flaming

and I met the poet Jason from the building next door
they've hit the pentagon someone yelled
and I went down to get some coffee
and when I came back one was down
wow I said to Jason
had I let go of you yet I can't remember

I went back to get some more
and none were left

I drink a lot less coffee now and I can sleep at night
but who could miss the flag like fourth of july
forever when they move the car
I think of it so much
when I ride over the manhattan bridge
on my bike or my car
when else do I look up
I never used to notice the towers

riding around Berlin This used to be a wall neighborhood
the wall was here, here, here
god they're haunted I thought
but where was it did I ever know
I just thought of it as 70s
and suppose it would've been nice to be a poet in residence
another grant I never got around to sending in

it was never out my window but I see it out there now

last night I thought about tripping
and the way the fags had yellow canvas deck chairs
and it was labor day and everyone was gone
it wasn't enough to sit on their furniture
at their little round table with the umbrella

we had this skid on the other side of the roof
they called it the dyke deck

and I remember lying there with our shirts off
so early in the morning
getting more and more sweet quarts of bud
writing with a soft pen
into the cheep industrial wood

more rebop

we thought fuck them
and threw the yellow deck chairs into the trees in the yard
they just hung there and we laughed and laughed
woke up thought oh no
there was a moment when they thought about evicting us
all the men

even the super Bill
who had some kind of anal cancer
an old marine who kept painting the foyer
you called it
the building's butt-hole

yellow and green
tan then brown
by the time he painted it horrible shiny silver
so bad when I was drunk
I thought what a goner
and yep he was dead soon

speaking of smells or halls tubes for living through

I think of Belansky:

Little Girl

mainly I think you just have to take the loss into account
I don't care if you get it

Little Girl

holes in my memory

sticking my hands in my jeans
jackets
which ones have the torn pockets
I repaired
and where do I put my keys
now
which pants am I in
do I remember them?

the bread must be saved
wrapped, protected
from age
because I am poor

and how am I to dress my flesh
if I'm not poor
anymore
how can I protect me from rotting
how can I allow

buy a new loaf everyday
throw it away
wildly fresh

Belansky who stunk
who never went out
hermit with a beard
and the stink poured when he opened
his door

little girl
go to the store for me
to buy baloney
and raisin bread
and two quarts of milk
for years
and keep the change

little girl

I'm 28
35
forty even forty
while he was still alive
some days walking really
slow past his door
I even knocked
I was so broke
I needed his forty cents

the day his stinky apartment was empty
now for years
the clean old man his brother
where were you all this time
when your brother had a beard
came to New York for something
grew inside here

FIFTY-THREE

I've already had a lot of them
I'm looking at a tree
full of tiny balls
California trees are different
thin eucalyptus more blades than
leaves not hitting
my face
it's a country of tiny leaves

no leaves

simply balls
I desire a big book about
this not better
than them but
their friend.
Who doesn't love the text?
a book about trees
it's like a park
except that all its windows
face outside
you look up at the world &
go: oh

a book is
a web I suppose

saying you come
here to go
out an
incessant
trembling bridge
which a tree
is
I imagine
a tree
my best friend
& I love
you on one
of so many birthdays

FOR JORDANA

I really do feel like
I am in some French
movie,
blam putting
down a general
cup of tea. The
lights are thus
and I squiggling
then returning
to my work
quietly squeezed
through the
day that's captured
some way
separately
not the squares
of the cinema
but envelopes
of affection

spea
spep
spe

separation

I think writing
is desire
not a form
of it. It's feeling
into space,
tucked into
language
slipped
into time,
opened,
felt. All this
as a matter

of course
of course

yet being
here somehow,
open

LODOVICO

The persimmons are mysterious;
they never get soft
I still don't believe
these are junipers
with their lonely commentary
a guy I know standing
outside.
Up a hill zips a car
its taillights on
going to work
whole parks are empty
in the morning
silent cause everyone's
gone to work
worse, & then I go!
But now I get
to stay home.
I like a whole long
Life of *here*
it's all I ever knew
alerting you & counting.
You who are blue.
I know the niceness
of silence. Hugged
up & tossled by dog
bark, its boxing pushing

of the silent morning
& then a bird gets
in there with
some adjusting &
a cat taps its head
against my thigh &
then settles in cat
pose in front of
a door & a porch
looking out & this
cat has never
gone out. I've been
squeezed into morning
& I take it. If
this is what I can
have. It starts
with the fruit that
never gets old &
that's mysterious
& next to them
are the dead.
The people who left
me this year; who
don't watch color
the point of our
maze. I've got

a pinecone like
a pineapple sitting
on my table. Interestingly
I look at nothing I
bought unless you
count this house
that I sit in.
I bought this view.
The dead bought out.
Of course I'll always
think of Heather
who leaned into
it. Such a willful
way to go. I remember
her leather coat.
And why am I standing
in June with her
family. To think boy
she really had money
& see her grave.
Heather chose to go
because of pain.
She felt chased out.
I also remember her
setting her back on
fire in a sex club.

Here's the part that's
insane. I dreamed
about it. Some
opportunity for all
of us to do so
to ourselves, just
for fun. It's like I already
know fire. I know
it inside. In my
dream I said
no or changed
the subject. Because
some people get
chased out &
some people are
taken out. I'm thinking
of Nancy who's
sick & doesn't want
to go. I called
Bob & he said
Eileen I'm dying.
Do I say Bye.
While the
cars keep curling
up the road,
I'm *here*.

It's a square
of a place
when the bed
chases me
awake
and the gleam
in the sky
that sweet curl
of white
says no. I've got
to live.

EACH DEFEAT

Please! Keep
reading me
Blake
because you're going to make
me the greatest
poet of
all time

Keep smoothing
the stones in the
driveway
let me fry an egg
on your ass
& I'll pick up
the mail.

I feel your
absence in
the morning
& imagine your
instant mouth
let me move
in with you—
Travelling
wrapping your limbs
on my back
I grow man woman
Child
I see wild wild wild

Keep letting the
day be massive
Unlicensed

Oh please have
my child
    I'm a little
    controlling
    Prose has some
    Magic. Morgan
had a
whore in
her lap. You
Big fisherman
I love my
Friends.

I want to lean
my everything
with you
make home for your hubris
I want to read the words you circld over and over again
A slow skunk walking across the road
Yellow, just kind
of pausing
picked up the warm
laundry. I just saw a coyote
tippy tippy tippy
I didn't tell you about the creature with hair
long hair, it was hit by cars on the highway
Again and again. It had long grey hair
It must've been a dog; it could've been
Ours. Everyone loses their friends.

I couldn't tell anyone about this sight.
Each defeat
Is sweet.

OOH

Baby's
apricot
with
its
tongue
hanging
out

I fight
the constant

conscious
conscious

I fight
for
you.

MOVIE

You're like
a little fruit
you're like
a moon I want
to hold
I said lemon slope
about your
hip
because it's one
of my words
about you
I whispered
in bed
this smoothing
the fruit &
then alone
with my book
but writing
in it the pages
wagging
against my knuckles
in the
light like a
sail.

Two animals, bears

    Her foot licking

mine

THERAPY

I like therapy because I don't need my glasses
I can sit there naked like the animal I am
a beautiful honest animal
a landscape of rolling reasons.
So amazing that an artist would use a cup
for a prayer; and no less amazing
that another animal would choose to be one
I considered being a cup
somewhere in my journey
between stars and thinking changing fonts was a revolution
standing in my green kitchen
Four years I've been to sea
so much is left on the old computer
things written in that place
one night getting rimmed
and then she fell asleep
spending hours mopping up the next day
in place of doing work
missing a party after all
I say always go to the party
which doesn't mean I do
some friends left early
I stayed and the sea spoke next

DEAR ANDREA

I love you too
don't fuck up my hair
I can't believe
you almost
fisted me
today.
That was great.
I see a little
duck's head.
Just separate—under the sand.
Are you really going
to read that.
I mean seriously
Honey. & the ocean
whooshes in.
Your jappy girlfriend.
K-toom.
Pouff. Ker-plash.
& rolling your pants
high. And the sea
hits the rocks &
the seagulls hop.
Man am I
in love.

DEAR ANDREA

I'm not trying
to turn you
on Eileen
I'm stretching
What time is it.
Twenty three before 6.
Dear God.
Should we feed them?
Oh yeah. I'm going
to take a shower
so let's do it now.
Are you done. How about
I take a shower
first. OK
I'd like you to
read me the
poem when
I'm done. What's that
Rose. Mm—err.

Nerr
Nerr?

DEAR ANDREA

I've been alone all
day. Spare me the postmodern
experimental poet
bullshit
Honey think hard
about moments of
love you've experienced
with me
I want that love.
Are we in a
relationship or not.
Eileen. Are you paying
attention

$50 for his ticket
$50 for his cat-case

These'll
Diesel

DEAR ANDREA

You are the candy melting
in my mouth.
Is that a euphemism
For what? Witnessing your love.
That's pretty good.
Oh I thought you said
Hear the candy
melting in my mouth.
All the people like me
are thanking all the people
like you. Can we call
it bird house?
I wouldn't take that
away from you. You're
like an orangutan.
You're like a little brother
I just allowed in
the bed. Did you
have coffee with
your dinner. No
I'm excited. We
bought a bird house
today. We didn't
get it yet. No
but we should
call it that. I. M.
sweet

UNNAMED NEW YORK

here in the beautiful
heat
digging & digging for
you
in your wide & wonderful
pause
day subway
de doggie
I was trying
to say it
writes
in bites
citizen aged local literary
queer cocksucking shop—
ping pussy
manifesting not
will Arnold win
if you enjoyed
smoking in bars
study French expressionism
employ your
loss
buy a car
take a course
make a college

buy something old
again & again
& again
the sneaker
swings
I like it here:

it's orange
& my hands are free.

The new book
was composed by picking shit
out of a wave.
Wherever they said vague
I thought vague

I couldn't help laughing
standing at the bottom
of my pit.
I thought Mark Twain was
here in the
crater of a giant
tomato
big artists like error.
The tomato
Missed.

Being intended
to hit god
it hit his mother
I speak for
her.

JACARANDA

What's
the feminine
of feet
I didn't
know I
could
have
a lavender
tree

you realize you have no
pants on as you're
walking down to the
pool
I have no pants on I
say
in this very unattractive
poem.
Your hair is wetly matting
your pubic bone & upper
thighs. I have to
get something
I tell my companion
and look there are
dogs
maybe this was just
before
as I'm playing over the
keys
of my fading dream.
One dog's really nice
little
the other dog poised
on a landing is bigger

& I get mad.
This one is for you.
I'm turning wildly
looking for newspaper
I realize I'm in
one of those dreams.
We've just showered
everything's perfect
when I say let's
go to the pool
and you agree
the warm pool
in this mysterious
public country
that has no head
no future. I have
no pen I'm
in bed
the shame of nakedness
how mad the dogs
made me, the
world is inside out
sounds on the street
(now gone)
in my new neighborhood
coming into sight

as the headless
country full of meaning
and you were there
with me
in my problem

always naked
fading
truth

HOME

It's not where I write
it's where I vegetate

—   —   —

a bathroom scale
on the sidewalk &
I step on
145 that can't be true
into the face
of a girl going by
She bows her head
don't make me know
what you know
don't make me see

I criticize the end
of a thought

more open gliding on

thru

on the 28th of April
heading back

Allen envied me
to just have
a life
[being in Russia
 as no one
 not him]

I love her anonymity
the marquee
from the dentist
chair the one little
rotten tooth
in a building

I write down
so I wake up

you probably think
I'm like
him too
busy to be

me but
I'm exactly
that
the tree

coming
back in a crack.

Lee Ann
I was ungenerous
standing on the
sidewalk looking
for them

I thought if
I inventoried home it would be broad
my eyes fling open
like a doll's
to the virtual space that suddenly
resembles the walls
the most interesting artists are large;
monsters
while the people we know are
masses of flowers
& when I turn
on my cellphone I see
everyone

holding my cell to the art
holding my cell at dinner
you guys: we're

all here.

It's like now that you've lived
with my mother
perhaps you
will enjoy
this imitation

in my writing class
the student
depicted the shrinkage
of her mom's
mom. It's so good
I said. The mortality
so affecting
creeping
them out
till I shrink
to a bone in my chair
you could use an outline
he said; I feel
you're just throwing

slam a pie in his face

are those pigeons
cooing down. Coo-

cone   cone   cone
"yeah my life"

CULTURE

It accepts all
marks & none
So I'll just write
into it
I spilt some tea
on your book
in California and the book
Is orange and black
America blasting next
door. Sometimes we like it;
sometimes we
don't. I'd like to buy one of those
really expensive
doors like I saw
in the Times
I like the sound
And they can
Give me that
Like it sounded in
Maine. The door of a boathouse
Could be mine. These women
didn't know anything
About doors
One made
Films and the other was
A nurse. I think they met

On a dock somewhere
Everything is a learning
Experience. Patty cake
is a dance. You
Don't think so. What's central is
Friendship. It really is.
Just try it on and it
Really works. Here it's
Idea, but it's perfect.
I don't think about
Getting better. I'm better
And a little worst.
Importantly I'm barely
Thinking in English. Like for instance
My celebration of nonething
almost killed
Me so I'd say
I'd qualify. I jumped on a plane
And I couldn't sleep
But I noticed the curtains
And pulled them shut
And it got better.
If I called her on time
It would'
Ve been great
But I woke up

Late so it didn't matter
Something had
Changed in her family.
Which is where important
Changes occur. I was
Open to the next
Experience but I
Couldn't get out. I climbed the fire escape
But the door on the roof
was locked. I called
Everyone from up there
Because I always
Have a
Phone and
Ellie called
Back hours later
Her mother's dying
So they can't
Move for a while
And I found a
Screwdriver and
Got out and arrived
in time
Breaking the no coffee
Rule. Okay I'm talking about an invisible
Culture. I wish I could help.

Service seems
Central, participation.
All this rushing to wind up
Walking down the street
Like the middle of the world
And later that night
It was dark and I remembered
Why I was dying to
Go. All these people
Are in trouble Every damn
One of them. First the buildings
Came down and now
They're all broke. I can't tell
Anymore if I am one
Of them but I moved
When I heard the bell.
Let's say I received
a call. We had a great dinner, so sweet.
Place called Dragonfly
And Linda kept being moved
I had invited her. It was easy.
I just did. Mostly I know
Men. I had many
More to see so I jumped in a car
At dawn to see my
Sister who interestingly

Was splashing around in a video
In a tube with little white glasses
On she wore them so early
She was cute. She looks like
Nancy. I know.
I looked so immigranty.
Like one of those pretty polish girls
In curlers. I was just one of the
Women in my family, the latest version
with my dimples and my
Food. Everyone in history
Should have videos of the past
So they can finally
Make the most irking
Connections of which
Ex-lovers look like
Which family friends
that you hate. My sister's house was like
Old single people with no children
I could stay here forever. Did you?
No. We're all getting our hands
In the dirt now. It's almost like in creation to creamation
Everyone has a desperate desire
To return to the earth
Now that we don't.
Lower me down.

I want it, seriously.
Living makes me hot.
Seems it would be time
For something foundation-
Al. All
These new words.
I'm barreling to the cape
In the rain. Car skids.
I think uh oh. Again and
again. Finally I'm at the gas tation
The reminds me of every
thing. The wing
Of the cape.
My big stupid
Boat. In Massachusetts
Where I know
All the people. Their adulthood
Scares me but
I must dip in. Arriving
The moment Marylyn
Has just opened
Her mouth
To close. She grins.
My silent connection.
I missed you.
I know. All day long I missed

Her calling and calling
just to let her
Know. Friendship. Knowing
I'd never get
There. It's like an ever-diving
Canyon, the love
Moving ahead,
green. I'm at larry's talking
About the male Nude.
What is it.
I don't know.
I realize
I don't want to fuck
them. No it's just
Where I sit.
Sleeping in the day
To go out and cavort.
Dinner over the
Work center. Noodles 'n
Clam, no scallop.
When I climb in
It's so fucking
Late but in the morning
We see the art
How come I can't remember—
Oh those.

Long as she's barking
I know it's not
Her mama. Funny we just haven't
Even connected. It makes me calm.
I know, I know.
Every time my father
Comes towards
me I cringe.
I can feel him cringing
At life.
All this racing
To produce
A greasy rat
Capable of being
Me. Barely
Alive. Too celebrated
Out to get
on the plane
So gone
I sicken
Myself
& hang
out

THAT COUNTRY

I've just
never known
what
to call
that country.
If I say
England
I don't think

I sound so
smart. I keep
tripping up
on their language which is English
so shouldn't their
country be the
same. Britain seems wrong,
does anyone
go to Britain?
People go to London
that's where they go.
There's really no country at all
just a city
huge, old
haven't been there for a while.
& UK is just a concept
a fashion statement

an economy
it seems you could have
a relationship
with that
but you wouldn't *go* there
you would allude.
Though, it includes everything,
doesn't it: the UK.
Ireland, Scotland,
England, all of it.
England is right

in there, but no place
else, which is why
I never say it.
But what about the
language they speak.
English. My penmanship
sharpens up. I go to
    school.
Slowly the words appear
on a line. Could I
write in that language
Think in it
Do I
am I missing something.

I really think a lot:
The second l in really
staggered into a y
the letters got
drunk. I wanted
to fuck up this
language & blame
its nameless
homeland:
the victors got drunk
they came & came
the words were never
the same again
in the last century
it came to us
to speak American
which means
to speak
where you land
which means
nothing now.
Not proud
but invasive.
Not the language
not the place
not them

not us
neither an island
nor a continent
nor a world
a spin without
a home.
An edgy
feeling. A coin
on its
side
speaking up

I'M MOVED

a squiggle of a river
becomes a road
in a play a boy
might walk
around a lot
and a woman
might be still.
Something in the water
might look like
brains
when the boy's
just sitting
there being
young; day
the moment might oc-
cur in memory
sentiment
I know musicians
know certain
chords do this
or that
we're a bunch
of turtles
when it comes
to feelings
the woman

is still and the
world around
her darkens
and we get
it—just
before the
boy started
walking. I wish the playwright
was brave.
to stay in that
corny suggestion
darkness
means
sadness
means time.
It's just our
burning star
and our
blue dirt
turning in its circle
a stand-in
for emotion
for scientists: you.
Who promised
to bring her
binoculars

somewhere, now here, to this grand

play. Just to

discover

art makes

me look

long & hard.

Why is light

so damn emotional

if it's just

a burning star.

This toe,

an inch

SCRIBBLE

Just let me
get these
flowers;
wrinkled, not
going
away. Remember
our party?
Or Lynne?
Lynne liked you so
much. See
her piece in
The Times,
you humming
while I write
Is it love
This must be punishment
you whistling
now
my blonde
my punishing
blonde
don't go

The deaf man
said
one tiny
little star
& that was
god, he
said.
OK let's talk.

THE FRAMES

In San Diego
where only the power
boxes
are painted
like art
I think the world
is a fucking mother
less
hole; flowers
scrambling around the
strong black
box.
I bought this
cd in Ireland.
It's a little morose
a little pretty
now I
learn it's
a hit
I wish
I were a boy
in England
not Irish
I wish I

was an American
knife
shiny
not
a life

SOMETHING SIMPLE

Thursday has not made
its mark
a week is inscription
a belt somewhere
your steps are riveted in my head
I am sympathetic
to all that's lost
the dog's bells
the shit pours
from the side of the house
all that's lost
is memory
London couldn't have
been so bad
in the fog
for instance
today hot & cold

NOW

There's something about
bad pens
that gives an air
of absolute insincerity
to everything—their caps off
'n the caps laying
around too
like shitty disciples
to the mess
I'm sorry I need to stay in my fog
& dictate these details
to no one
like a dog outside
bipping up going no mommy I hear
dictator of the mess
secretary of a dog's clicking
nails
which float across our sea
like degrees
along a thermometer
laying flat numbers
ushering everything into a room
I can see
do you hate me now
Darling I want nothing but this

endless flow
of getting loose
then holding my bear
alone on the couch
& it's you

SAN DIEGO POEM

the jacarandas turn on like lights
city heights is in fact beautiful
guided by voices
disturbs me however
I will get to the 15
going north to Adams
to return disc 2
of Brazil
I hated it when it came out
the same
thing I always hate
dirty like Kienholzes
like dirty technology
the midwest
which is like London
somehow greasy
who gets British humor
I can't
I think of my dad
who purportedly liked
sex so much
in fact sex in this
town
did he ever know
his little kid would

teach college
here pull over under
purple trees
to think about him

& the urge

CIGARETTE GIRL

a long rain
drop more
of a tear
fell from
an awning or a nail
shit the top
of a roof
and hit my neck
inside my
coat
I don't know
how it got
in so perfectly
& struck
my flesh
my warm
white neck
on a rainy
night in
winter
I almost
said this to you

she wanting
to move on

if I spoke
another language
I'd break into
it now
there's nothing
lonelier
than a lonely
American
my limits
contract &
expand

I grab the white
handle of
my speech
like it's an
umbrella
and I shake
it free
of words
empty American
balloon
holy smoke

looking out
at the
street
it's nothing
to know
you, puff

TO HELL

for J.

I'm not sure who I walk with in America today.

I miss you, my imagined accomplice, while we're
         moving among men

One man stands up and says his daughter's gay

Like we didn't know that she says, he thinks it's so great

We can't think it's so wonderful, being lied to for years

We've accomplished bright cynicism, then struggle for love

We flounder, we fail, the elephant eliminates the con-
         fusions of love.

Love probably didn't need a war, couldn't eat, is rolling
         on waves today

The city is emptying. The elephants have been planning
         their party for years.

I'm heading into it. New York my home bursting with men.

Conservative women, heading downtown to see a cross made
         of girders: "Great!"

Jesus marked this city, threw planes at it, face it those
         pilots were gay

We're gonna make a constitutional amendment against em
for being gay.

Gay to hit buildings, to want to meet in great numbers,
being no one Love

Moving like an angry sunflower, wanting bandages, space,
something great

I want to live here feeling celebrated for breathing open
today.

I want to show you complicated dyke love, construct a poem
about women and men

In my country there's a basic responsibility to struggle
and not for years.

To walk away, to turn around seeing you and progress and be
loving your smile for years

Sometimes I think there's complication with men but I'm
probably gay

Gay to be glad to keep expressing and knowing the im-
possible hopes of women and men

I would want to learn more, be firmer, open up, revolutionize
love streaming

A house on a hill is pretty but there's something
rhapsodically fine today

Stay here while the American ship is moving and rocking,
vincible, great.

My moment alone in front of everyone is hopelessly great

I don't have to wonder where I'm going this time or this
year

I don't have to wonder whose group I'm in today.

Certainly the people who always think the public problem is
theirs are gay

When the moment comes to move like trees to free the city I
love

I don't know John Kerry and we can name that feeling Bud-
dhist for the next four years

The pond reflects the sky, if the highway curls it's gay.

A public moment, a political moment is what's possible
today

We trust more than men, something's eating our years

The uneven horizon's great and of course she's gay

The buildings are falling in love, and we opened its eye
today

I don't mind today, but the everyday makes me barf. There's no such thing. Puking would put something on the sidewalk of the everyday so it might begin to be now. And what do we think about writing now. I was asked to write a political sestina for someone and once I did they sent it back all numbered and pointing out I had not done it correctly. Not only had I not gotten correctly to the envoi, but harrumph I had also done something with the six words, something bad. I had never written a sestina before and I was fairly proud of it. After a few pissy exchanges I was declared hateful by this guy because I suggested he was conservative and even censorious. It simply strikes me that form has a real honest engagement with content and therefore might even need to get a little sleazy with it suggesting it stop early or go too far. How can you stop form from wanting to do that. I wrote my sestina on a boat. I was living in P-town this summer in Mimi's house where she often pointed out that Charles (Bernstein) had also lived with his family. Each time I left that house to go to New York or California I took a quick boat and this one time it was the week of the RNC and I thought well I'll write the fucking sestina on the way to the reading in New York. It's a political reading, so I'm thinking that way. The boat bucked and rocked. I thought the poem was incredibly boring, the words forced but for some reason I had nothing better to do I kept plodding along, peeking at my scheme. I was teaching a workshop that week at FAWC; do you know what FAWC is.

Later in New York I was standing outside of Fox (unrelated) with a group of activists and we were screaming get the Fox out of here. Get—the—Fox out of here. Then we would go: O-Reil-ly. O-Reil-ly. This Bronx cheer that made me a little nervous. Certainly O'Reilly's a conservative prick but are they laughing at him for being Irish. Are they invoking some working class dialect, some familiarity or something because of the sound of his name. I have never watched this guy. Does he play the regular guy? What's his voice like? Who are the activists who have written the cheer. I was glad when they went back to the Fox one. Get the Fox out of here!

The experience of arriving at an activist event you've only read about—one you've selected from an online calendar of them. And maybe by now standing there with your friends. Holding a hot pink unemployment sheet. Standing in Union Sq. knowing that a line of you reaches down to Wall Street and up to Penn Station. Just being an arm in a performance piece. Just being a voice, like being in some weeklong workshop all over New York against the republican party and you can just kind of dip in. When O'Reilly got in trouble recently I thought about standing outside his job yelling his name. I mean I didn't feel bad or anything but now there was a release—like whatever discomfort I'd been feeling now slammed up against a good solid scandal so the screaming at last felt right.

The boat jogged my poem and I got to New York and read it in a large room and it was hot and I felt like I had done my poet job. I sat back down with J—, increasingly my ex who nodded and squeezed my arm. "You did good." I took the boat again a few weeks later. I was feeling a little sad this time since I had been trying to get my mother who lives in Massachusetts to come back with me to P-town, but maybe I really didn't want that, and she didn't know if she wanted that either, but somehow I now felt I had failed. The boat bucked and waved. The boat was rocking so badly that finally no one was allowed to be out on the deck. They had to come in. I saw a girl out there in a hood with her boyfriend. Maybe her hood was gold. I had one of those. I used to wear it under a tweed suitjacket. Or maybe it was *his* sweatshirt that was gold. Was it raining. It was stormy. It was almost too stormy for people to ride boats. And the man next to me began puking. Urp, he went. Splatter, right into a paper bag. I think he was a fag. He was with his lover. Wha Wha Wha. He gagged. The woman next to me & I looked slightly at each other. This is gross. She was sitting with a man, but she chose me to share the feeling with. We were disgusted. Maybe a little bit scared. I didn't want to puke. Not like this. No place. I never want to puke. Hate puking. Haven't puked for years. Then behind me a woman began. Really gagging her ass off. Heaving. Again, and again. Little coughs of puke. Getting it together. Puking again. We were sick. The whole bunch of us were rocking with the gags, praying to fucking god we wouldn't start puking our guts out too. You could also smell the stuff. And the rain splashing against the glass windows of the boat. The boat tipping, aiming up. Have you noticed how tipping is in the news. For a while things were spiking, they were ramping up and now they're tipping. That's the word we like, it's what we see and I saw the boat rolling and tipping. Barf. It seemed my mother wouldn't have enjoyed this trip. She's 83. How would she receive a boat full of puking adults. I think she would have gotten up and moved. She wouldn't have just sat there. I began to think I had done the right thing by not getting her on this boat with me. I wasn't so wrong. Opened my notebook and started celebrating the fact. What fact. My séance. My sitting there on my ass on the boat in the middle of all these people puking. You think of kids, I always heard that kids in you know like first grade have this serial puking. I hear it as a story in families too. Suddenly each kid one after another started puking their guts out. Mom and Dad mopping up, occasionally lowering their own heads into the toilet. Blah. Adults do it too. I imagine my relatives coming over from Europe puking on the floor of the boat in between fucks and bites of jerky. Bites of their belts or their shoes. Whatever they ate. Sucking on the tittie. Whatever. From this primal scene I wrote my mother a poem. The puking I do. This. Dear Mom. Blah. My whole life shooting all over the windows of the boat. Dear Mom Blah. The stuff streaming word by word across the lines dripping down the page of my notebook. A black and white composition notebook. One of those spray theme covers with a nice rectangle of ownership saying who I am. Eileen. This is my book. Dear Mom. I stopped apologizing for not bringing her. I understood she would have gotten sick. There was a logic. Perhaps I'll read the poem. In it I shared my fear of dying with my mother. There's a kind of dying that lives in my family. An accidental clown death. My father died like that. Fell off the roof. Splat. I think I had just been robbed in Los Angeles. I had been at the delightful Pho café in a crowd of art people standing around rubbing their bellies satisfied while another crowd popped my trunk and stole my computer and all my clothes including my new digital camera I hadn't figured out yet. Utterly gone. There's one of those 30-second videos on it. Me standing inside my camera telling a joke. My trunk's wide open like a complete asshole. Nobody noticed it happen except me. I was poking my head out the door of the restaurant and there's my trunk wide open. I'm not upset. I'm numb. I'm a little destroyed. I got my notebook, I continued my dinner with Simon. Later that night I went to Judith's where I was staying and though she told me she lived upstairs the downstairs door was open and I walked right in. It looked wrong; the art, something. Suddenly this guy is coming towards me, scared. Scared like he would pick up a gun and shoot me he was so scared. Dear Mom, not only have I drowned today, but I was robbed and then I was shot. Bad luck. All these thoughts teeming as people around me go whaa. It hasn't stopped. It's normalized. Once my girlfriend moved to Paris, like 1986, and I took her to the airport. Then I got on the train I think and went home. It was a big deal but I wasn't upset. I walked into the bathroom and began shitting and puking at once. I felt like a worm. Like there was no difference between me—and anything. It was just this force flowing through me. Loss. I must be feeling bad I thought, sitting on the can leaning into the sink. What must I be feeling. She had wanted to go to Acme, a restaurant on Jones St. What did we eat. Chicken fried steak. Maybe that's what it was. In my poem I start telling my mother about the kids outside the window. I guess I was writing my poem throughout the puking. I even tried to read. There was this great book Chronophobia which was about time. Like what's not, right. I can barely tell you what it was about yet I feel all these systems kicking in. Like when you hear your computer shift. The book was just so right. People driving in cars on unborn highways, people blowing things up in deserts. A woman Bridget Riley going to see a collector who turned her work into a dress. I thought you'd like it, he said. She got blamed for Op Art which they continually tried to link to her being some kind of Irish domestic servant, and she responded by negating her sex. Feminism was splashing up around her like vomit and obviously that's the problem. I remember in junior high we would walk across the street to the high school to get our lunch. One kid would hold the door open for hundreds of others and that kid would announce every day what it was. He said, vomit. The door was reddish kind of clay colored. He stood on a cement block and it made him taller than us while he held the door. I remember thinking oh vomit for lunch. I didn't know what that was. We would "throw up" when I was a kid, that's what we did at home and maybe around 6th grade the word *puke* came in. This is like 1961. I sat down at the lunch table with my orange tray. On the plate was a pile of little brown meatballs in a light brown gravy. In retrospect I guess it was Swedish meatballs. I think that would be its name. I ate the little meatballs. They were not bad. We got back to class and the nun asked us what we had had for lunch and I said *vomit* quickly, feeling smart at once. A new Swedish word. I remember standing out in the hall that afternoon, being punished for *the word*, remembering the raucous sound of the classroom laughter. Even I joined in, feeling entirely out of control, humiliated, but the enormous release the one word had triggered still made me snort and gag with pleasure. Alone. It wasn't so bad to be totally wrong if you just didn't know and it was so much fun. There was something Bob Dylan didn't know and I can't remember what it was. It was about moving. I totally devoured that book, his autobiography. Amra asked me what I had been seeing lately. Like what was my art month. It was the show at the Hammer, I liked that painting show, The Undiscovered Country. I suppose I liked the title more than the show. I mean I liked the show. But the idea of a painting show being named after death seems just brilliant. I mean it's so fucking coy. Is painting really so far away. From who? It's just a crazy idea, but Shakespeare's line is so damn good that you can hang anything on it and it works. Bob Dylan said if you write while you're moving, it's good. The painting becomes really alive in the land of dead words. In the dream of death. Death is so great because it's the attachment you can never open. I mean you can force it open, but is that really yours. I saw Tarnation and I'm not sure what I think. Who could not love that kid doing drag at twelve or thirteen. Who was not scared for that kid. But the whole story was not a good idea. I hate the whole story. I hate it with a passion. Which is why I loved Bob Dylan's book. I had been prepared by another idea I had about him. J__ gave me Positively Fourth Street this other Bob Dylan book and I thought why do you think I care about that but this summer in P-town I simply read one book after another that she gave me. It's hard to live with someone *and* read the books they give you. You'd rather ask them why they gave it to you and be done with it. Though in their absence you read. Bob Dylan used to tear pictures out of magazines and arrange them on the floor and then kneel over them with his guitar and write songs. It seems so perfect. Now that I think about it it seems like jerking off. I'm not sure if it's jerking off like a man. It might be jerking off like a woman. In his own book Chronicles, Bob describes coming to New York and hanging out and singing his songs. I mean he was singing other people's songs for a while. I think his first song he pretended it was somebody else's and he slipped it in with theirs.

He loved Woody Guthrie and he went to see him every day in the hospital when Woody was dying. It seems like a man thing to do, to visit the great guy dying. I really don't know who the great woman is, so where would I go. My mother would always try and make us look at the sky. Look at that sunset Eileen. It made you really want to look away. It just ruined it for me. It was all about her. And that's what I saw when I looked out the window that day. All these words were living. The boat was rocking and the people were puking and it was her gift to me. So I say what our president said when he was told how great it was to have god in the white house. He said thank you. He thanked them for how beautiful they were. It was good to be here.

Acknowledgments

Some of these poems have appeared in the following journals, anthologies and websites: *The American Poetry Review, Aphros, Baffling Combustions, Best American Poetry 2004, Bloom, Caffeine Destiny, Columbia Poetry Review 19, Ecstatic Peace Journal, effing 4, Electronic Poetry Review, Gargoyle 50, Mississippi Review, New American Writing, Open City, Shiny, Superflux, Time Out New York, Van Gogh's Ear,* and *The Outlaw Bible of American Essays.*

"Everyday Barf" was written to present at a panel (on the poetry of everyday) at Séance at RedCat (2004). I thank all these great editors, curators and friends.